PERFECT CUSTOMER
Who has your money?

By Matt Bacak

IMPORTANT LEGAL STUFF

If you would like to get your hands on the templates used inside this book, please go right now to
www.perfectcustomerbook.com/freetemplates

Credits

Managing Editor, Cover/Graphic
Design/Illustration, Layout:

Christopher L. May

If you would like to get your hands on the templates used inside this
book, please go right now to
www.perfectcustomerbook.com/freetemplates

If you would like to get your hands on the templates used inside this book, please go right now to
www.perfectcustomerbook.com/freetemplates

PERFECT CUSTOMER

According to the SBA (Small Business Administration), 95% of small businesses fail within the first 5 years. One of the main reasons these businesses fail is the lack of a clearly defined target audience. If asked, many small business owners will say that their target audience is stay at home moms, college students, or middle-aged men. The problem is that those demographics are way too general of an audience for the end result to be profitable.

Some will even say that they don't have a specific target audience. That their products or services are for everyone.

That's a mistake that is all too familiar to thousands of aspiring entrepreneurs. Because when you try to target everyone, you're speaking to no one. You're simply wasting time and money and you're not likely to see any return for all your hard work.

You cannot successfully market and grow your business if you don't understand who your perfect customer is. If you don't know exactly who you are talking to, how can you expect to reach them?

If you would like to get your hands on the templates used inside this book, please go right now to
www.perfectcustomerbook.com/freetemplates

It's like trying to call someone without knowing their phone number.

Using generic terms and language in marketing material is not going to make your products and/or services stand out from the millions of others on the market.

To guarantee your marketing efforts are targeted and much more cost effective, you need to create your perfect customer avatar, or persona,. Profiling that customer who needs your products and/services the most will allow you to craft your marketing messages to stand out and appeal to him or her directly. Your perfect customer will return repeatedly, spend more money, and recommend you to friends and family. This customer will be amazing to do business with and will generate a large percentage of your profit.

Sounds great, right?

Let's get started now by completing my 6 step formula which will allow you to profile your perfect customer and create his or her avatar.

If you would like to get your hands on the templates used inside this book, please go right now to
www.perfectcustomerbook.com/freetemplates

How to Create Your Perfect Customer Avatar

Having a clear understanding of who your perfect customer is allows you to stop spending time and money advertising to the wrong audience. Instead, you can focus on creating content and copy that really connects with your perfect customers. The most successful entrepreneurs create a connection with customers by showing that they are relatable. Research shows that an emotional connection plays a key role in a buyer's purchasing decisions.

Most people resonate with movie characters, characters from books, celebrities (which in most cases are carefully crafted personas), and actors in general. It's human nature. People will usually give a quick glance at the "characters" they see in commercials without giving it much thought. Although a lot of money, and I mean A LOT of money goes into creating those characters and mascots. Think of Flo from Progressive, the Pine-Sol lady, or "The Most Interesting Man in the World"...

One particular Canadian Ad campaign that sticks out in my memory is, Jay "The Strong Silent Type"

If you would like to get your hands on the templates used inside this book, please go right now to
www.perfectcustomerbook.com/freetemplates

from McCain's' Superfries (You Can Find The Commercial On YouTube); they nailed it with that ad campaign and kept running different ads with "Jay" because it worked so well; we often think of them as stereotypes and thinking of your customer avatar in the same way will help you shape your avatar into something people can identify with.

I want to give you a very easy method for you to create your own "Customer Avatar" in a way that makes your marketing speak directly to your customers "needs" "likes" and "wants" in a way that creates good will and happy, happy, happy customers. The kind that don't refund, the kind that wait for your next product or want to use your services over and over again (or refer their friends and coworkers.) A lot of this will be familiar to you if you read or write any sales copy, but in my experience people are really just copying and pasting what they see other people do and don't have an understanding of what really makes a particular sentence impactful. Either that or they use a really powerful piece in the wrong place or merely use it to make the features and benefits sound "pretty" instead of relating them to a particular 'customer avatars' life situation by weaving your product or services features and benefits into his/her needs, likes and wants.

If you would like to get your hands on the templates used inside this book, please go right now to
www.perfectcustomerbook.com/freetemplates

Doing it in this way allows you to show how your product or service can fulfill their strongest needs and by doing so they will get what they want in a way they like.

The purpose and goal behind this book is to create a customer avatar and to teach you how to use that customer avatar to help people understand when and where to use certain language patterns. The aim is to understand how and why avatars work and to understand that it isn't so much about selling a product or service to someone, but to creating an experience that provides the results that they desire. We will accomplish this by using a system that can streamline the entire process and make it less confusing, more imaginative, and creative. By creating a customer avatar this way we'll be able to laser target their needs, wants and likes to your product or services features and benefits.

This book will lay out a series of 6 exercises to help you create your customer avatar which will specifically targets the needs, wants and likes and connect them to the features and benefits of your products (or affiliate products) and services in such a way that makes it effortless to create persuasive

If you would like to get your hands on the templates used inside this book, please go right now to
www.perfectcustomerbook.com/freetemplates

copy by taking all the guessing out of your writing process.

Step #1: We'll start by answering at least 30 questions from the Customer Avatar Questions exercise, although I recommend spending as much time getting as detailed as you can

Customer Avatar Questions

- Common Fears, Frustrations, Pain, Urgency

- Wants & Aspirations

- Common Experiences, Reality

- Common Irrational Fears & Fantasies

- Name & Describe Your Avatar to Bring To Life

The top 30 questions should be all you need to start with your customer avatar, but I wanted to include a good source for questions which you can use to generate more content if you get stuck. Some of these questions can be a great basis to start

If you would like to get your hands on the templates used inside this book, please go right now to
www.perfectcustomerbook.com/freetemplates

formulating a video or marketing campaign, because you can speak to a specific trait or bias as though it's a real person you know instead of trying to make everything up with no context. Having a customer avatar makes it much easier and more natural to write.

It's a lot easier to convince someone you "know." You naturally use persuasive language patterns in your daily life with people you know, so the idea here is to create your ideal customer as someone who is REALLY familiar to you, almost like a friend or family member.

You can start with the first 30 questions and write the answers down in point form so you can reference them later where we'll begin to relate them to your product or services benefits and features.

Answer the rest of the questions as you go along "getting to know" your Customer Avatar better personally; this process will make it easier to write convincing persuasive copy; the idea behind all of this is to build your avatar as you would naturally build a relationship with a real person.

We're going to relate your Customer Avatar to your products or services benefits and features to find

If you would like to get your hands on the templates used inside this book, please go right now to
www.perfectcustomerbook.com/freetemplates

out the common need that your product or service will fulfill for them so we can tailor our final marketing pieces to speak directly to that strong need(s). Speaking directly to their needs will convert them like crazy, especially in today's marketing world because you can target certain demographics of people very specifically based on a wide variety of variables like sex and age, location and in some cases even income, it just makes sense to create a Customer Avatar so using those variables when you market becomes relevant (they're there for a reason, right?).

One quick method for finding common Needs/Wants/Likes in your niche (if you're stuck) is to look at posts related to your niche and to check the questions people ask about the Product / Service then you have a basic framework for the types of things that are important to the people in your particular niche. Write down their questions and any other information they've provided and integrate it into your customer avatar.

If you would like to get your hands on the templates used inside this book, please go right now to
www.perfectcustomerbook.com/freetemplates

30 Questions for Your Avatar

1. SEX, AGE & NAME
2. MARITAL STATUS / RELATIONSHIP STATUS
3. DO THEY HAVE KIDS
4. CURRENT JOB SITUATION & MONTHLY INCOME
5. CURRENT LIVING SITUATION (HOUSE OR APARTMENT, RENTAL OR MORTGAGE, LIVING CONDITIONS [CLEAN OR DIRTY, REQUIRES REPAIR, BRAND NEW ETC.]
6. PEOPLE IN THEIR DAILY LIVES; SPOUSE, CHILDREN, FRIENDS, PETS, ACQUAINTANCES ETC.
7. WHAT DO THEY EAT DAILY; BREAKFAST, LUNCH AND DINNER
8. WHAT IS THEIR PHYSICAL APPEARANCE LIKE? SHOWER DAILY? UNSHAVEN, SHAVEN? MAKEUP, NO MAKEUP?
9. ARE THEY LAZY OR MOTIVATED?
10. WHAT DO THEY DO FOR FUN? HOW DO THEY UNWIND?
11. WHAT KIND OF TELEVISION SHOWS DO THEY WATCH? WHAT KIND OF MOVIES?

If you would like to get your hands on the templates used inside this book, please go right now to
www.perfectcustomerbook.com/freetemplates

12. WHAT KIND OF BOOKS WOULD THEY / DO THEY READ? WHAT KIND OF MAGAZINES GET THEIR INTEREST
13. WHAT KIND OF MUSIC DO THEY LISTEN TO?
14. ARE THEY NEW TO INTERNET MARKETING?
15. HOW MUCH DO THEY KNOW ABOUT THE NICHE / SERVICE
16. ARE THEY JUST STARTING OUT, DO THEY KNOW A BIT, OR ARE THEY PROFESSIONALS?
17. IF THEY'RE MARRIED, WHAT IS THE SPOUSE LIKE?
18. WHAT DOES THE SPOUSE THINK OF ALL THIS FOOLISHNESS?
19. WHAT'S THE RELATIONSHIP WITH THE CHILDREN LIKE?
20. WHAT WOULD THIS PERSON BE WEARING?
21. WHAT IS THEIR BIGGEST FRUSTRATION?
22. WHAT IS THEIR BIGGEST SURFACE DESIRE?
23. WHAT ARE THEY CURRENTLY TRYING TO ACCOMPLISH?
24. WHERE DO THEY LIKE TO WORK
25. HOW DO THEY LIKE TO WORK
26. WHAT IS THEIR BIGGEST FEAR / FRUSTRATION
27. WHAT IS THEIR COMMON REALITY
28. WHAT ARE THEY EMBARRASSED TO ADMIT TO THEMSELVES
29. WHAT IS THE CONVERSATION GOING ON IN THEIR HEAD
30. WHAT DO THEY DRIVE?
31. WHERE DO THEY WANT TO BE IN 5 YEARS?

If you would like to get your hands on the templates used inside this book, please go right now to
www.perfectcustomerbook.com/freetemplates

32. HOW ARE YOU, REALLY?
33. HOW DO YOU FEEL RIGHT NOW? WHAT ARE YOU THINKING ABOUT?
34. WHAT'S YOUR FAVORITE COLOR?
35. WHAT'S YOUR FAVORITE FOOD?
36. WHAT'S YOUR FAVORITE DESSERT?
37. HOW OLD ARE YOU?
38. WHAT HAVE YOU LEARNED TODAY?
39. WHAT WAS YOUR FAVORITE SUBJECT IN SCHOOL?
40. WHAT DO YOU DO?
41. WHAT ARE SOME OF YOUR FAVORITE BOOKS?
42. WHAT ARE SOME OF YOUR FAVORITE MOVIES?
43. WHAT KIND OF MUSIC ARE YOU INTO?
44. IF YOU WERE GOING TO WRITE A BOOK, WHAT WOULD YOU CALL IT AND WHAT WOULD IT BE ABOUT?
45. WHAT'S ONE OF THE SCARIEST THINGS YOU'VE EVER DONE?
46. WHAT ACCOMPLISHMENT ARE YOU MOST PROUD OF?
47. ARE YOU MARRIED?
48. HOW DID YOU MEET YOUR SPOUSE / GIRLFRIEND / BOYFRIEND?
49. DO YOU THINK IT'S BETTER TO GET MARRIED WHEN YOU'RE YOUNG OR BETTER TO WAIT A WHILE?
50. DO YOU HAVE ANY KIDS?
51. HAVE YOU EVER THOUGHT OF ADOPTING?
52. WHEN YOU WERE A KID, WHAT DID YOU WANT TO BE WHEN YOU GREW UP?

If you would like to get your hands on the templates used inside this book, please go right now to
www.perfectcustomerbook.com/freetemplates

53. How did you get into [INSERT THEIR CAREER FIELD]?
54. Would you recommend [INSERT THEIR CAREER] for other people? Why / Why not?
55. What do you do for fun?
56. Do you like traveling?
57. If you could visit any country in the world, where would you go?
58. Who are some people you'd like to meet someday?
59. If someone asked you to give them a random piece of advice, what would you say?
60. What's one of your favorite habits you have?
61. What are some things that make you really happy?
62. What are some things that make you really sad?
63. What are some things that scare you?
64. Do you like to plan things out in detail or be spontaneous?
65. Are you a religious person?
66. If you could go back in history, who would you like to meet?
67. Would you rather live in the country or in the city?
68. What was your life like growing up?
69. What were you like in high school?
70. Do you have any brothers or sisters? How many?

If you would like to get your hands on the templates used inside this book, please go right now to
www.perfectcustomerbook.com/freetemplates

71. WHAT'S YOUR FAVORITE PART ABOUT TODAY SO FAR?
72. WHO IN YOUR LIFE HAS INFLUENCED YOU THE MOST? HOW DID THEY DO IT?
73. WHAT'S YOUR FAVORITE JOKE?
74. HAVE YOU EVER TRIED SUSHI? (DID YOU LIKE IT?)
75. DO YOU LIKE SPICY FOOD?
76. HOW DO YOU LIKE YOUR STEAK COOKED?
77. DO YOU HAVE A FAVORITE NUMBER? ANY PARTICULAR REASON WHY YOU LIKE THAT NUMBER?
78. IF YOU WERE A TYPE OF ANIMAL, WHAT WOULD YOU BE AND WHY?
79. WHAT'S ONE OF THE STRANGEST THINGS YOU'VE EVER DONE?
80. WHAT KIND OF VACATIONS DO YOU LIKE?
81. WHAT ARE SOME OF YOUR MAJOR GOALS IN LIFE?
82. WHAT ARE SOME OF YOUR SMALLER GOALS IN LIFE?
83. WHAT DO YOU LIKE LEAST ABOUT YOURSELF?
84. WHAT EMBARRASSES YOU?
85. IF YOU COULD TRY OUT ANY JOB FOR A DAY, WHAT WOULD YOU LIKE TO TRY?
86. WHAT'S YOUR EARLIEST MEMORY?
87. WHAT'S THE BEST DECISION YOU EVER MADE?
88. WHO'S YOUR BEST / CLOSEST FRIEND?
89. WHAT DO YOU THINK PEOPLE THINK OF YOU?
90. WHAT WERE YOUR GRADES LIKE IN SCHOOL?
91. IF YOU COULD LEARN ONE RANDOM SKILL, WHAT WOULD YOU LEARN?

If you would like to get your hands on the templates used inside this book, please go right now to
www.perfectcustomerbook.com/freetemplates

92. ARE YOU AN INTROVERT OR AN EXTROVERT?
93. HAVE YOU EVER TAKEN A PERSONALITY TEST? (HOW DID THE RESULTS TURN OUT?)
94. WHAT'S THE FIRST THING YOU NOTICE ABOUT PEOPLE?
95. DO YOU THINK PEOPLE CAN CONTROL THEIR OWN DESTINY?
96. DO YOU THINK ALL PEOPLE ARE EQUALLY VALUABLE, OR DO YOU THINK SOME PEOPLE IN CERTAIN SITUATIONS MIGHT BE MORE VALUABLE THAN OTHERS (SAY, A SEVERELY RETARDED PATIENT VS.? A DOCTOR WHO COULD POTENTIALLY SAVE HUNDREDS OF LIVES)?
97. DO YOU THINK PEOPLE ARE BASICALLY BAD OR BASICALLY GOOD?
98. DO YOU THINK MORALS ARE UNIVERSAL OR RELATIVE TO THE BELIEFS, TRADITIONS, AND PRACTICES OF INDIVIDUALS OR GROUPS?
99. DO YOU THINK GOD EXISTS?
100. DO YOU THINK ANY KIND OF AFTERLIFE EXISTS?
101. DO YOU VOTE? WHY / WHY NOT? IF YOU DO VOTE, HOW DO YOU USUALLY VOTE?
102. DO YOU THINK GAY PEOPLE CHOOSE TO BE GAY? DO YOU THINK STRAIGHT PEOPLE CHOOSE TO BE STRAIGHT?
103. IS TORTURE EVER A GOOD OPTION? IF NO, WHY NOT? IF YES, WHEN?
104. WOULD YOU KILL AN INNOCENT PERSON IF YOU THOUGHT IT MIGHT MEAN SAVING A DOZEN OTHER PEOPLE?

If you would like to get your hands on the templates used inside this book, please go right now to
www.perfectcustomerbook.com/freetemplates

105. WHAT'S THE MOST MONEY YOU'VE EVER GIVEN AWAY?
106. WHAT'S THE BIGGEST PERSONAL CHANGE YOU'VE EVER MADE?
107. WHAT'S THE STUPIDEST THING YOU'VE EVER DONE?
108. WHAT DO YOU THINK WOULD BE ONE OF THE BEST STEPS WE COULD TAKE TOWARD ENDING POVERTY AROUND THE WORLD?
109. WHAT DO YOU THINK WE COULD DO TO BEST IMPROVE THE EDUCATION SYSTEM?
110. IN GENERAL, WHAT DO YOU THINK ABOUT ART?
111. WHAT ARE SOME OF YOUR FAVORITE WEBSITES?
112. WHAT'S THE BIGGEST TURNOFF IN A MAN/WOMAN?
113. WHAT'S THE BIGGEST LIE YOU'VE EVER TOLD?
114. WHAT'S SOMETHING MOST PEOPLE DON'T KNOW ABOUT YOU?
115. WHAT'S SOMETHING YOU WISH EVERYONE KNEW ABOUT YOU?
116. WHAT ARE SOME OF THE FIRST THINGS YOU DO IN THE MORNING?
117. WHAT'S THE WORST THING THAT'S EVER HAPPENED TO YOU?
118. DO YOU CRY EASILY?
119. HOW DO YOU FEEL ABOUT PUBLIC SPEAKING?
120. DO YOU LIKE TO TALK ON THE PHONE?
121. HOW MANY EMAILS DO YOU GET EACH WEEK, ROUGHLY?

If you would like to get your hands on the templates used inside this book, please go right now to
www.perfectcustomerbook.com/freetemplates

122. IF SOMEONE WERE TO MAKE A MOVIE ABOUT YOUR LIFE, WHO WOULD YOU HOPE WOULD PLAY YOU?
123. WHAT'S ONE OF YOUR FAVORITE QUESTIONS TO ASK NEW FRIENDS OR TO GET A CONVERSATION GOING?
124. WOULD YOU EVER SKY DIVE OR BUNGEE JUMP?
125. HAVE YOU EVER BEEN IN A FIST FIGHT?
126. WHAT'S THE BEST PRANK YOU'VE EVER PULLED?
127. WHAT DID YOU DO ON YOUR 16TH BIRTHDAY?
128. WHAT DO YOU THINK IS ONE OF THE MOST UNDERVALUED PROFESSIONS RIGHT NOW?
129. HOW WOULD YOU EXPLAIN YOUR BASIC LIFE PHILOSOPHY?
130. WOULD YOU RATHER BE HATED OR FORGOTTEN?
131. IF YOU KNEW YOU WOULD DIE TOMORROW, WOULD YOU FEEL CHEATED TODAY?
132. WHAT WAS YOUR FAVORITE FOOD WHEN YOU WERE A CHILD?
133. WHAT'S THE #1 MOST PLAYED SONG ON YOUR IPOD?
134. WHAT IS ONE OF YOUR FAVORITE QUOTES?
135. WHAT'S YOUR FAVORITE INDOOR/OUTDOOR ACTIVITY?
136. WHAT CHORE DO YOU ABSOLUTELY HATE DOING?
137. WHAT IS YOUR FAVORITE FORM OF EXERCISE?
138. WHAT IS YOUR FAVORITE TIME OF DAY/DAY OF THE WEEK/MONTH OF THE YEAR?

If you would like to get your hands on the templates used inside this book, please go right now to
www.perfectcustomerbook.com/freetemplates

139. WHAT'S YOUR LEAST FAVORITE MODE OF TRANSPORTATION?
140. WHAT IS YOUR FAVORITE BODY PART?
141. WHAT SOUND DO YOU LOVE?
142. IF YOU COULD THROW ANY KIND OF PARTY, WHAT WOULD IT BE LIKE AND WHAT WOULD IT BE FOR?
143. IF YOU COULD PAINT A PICTURE OF ANY SCENERY YOU'VE SEEN BEFORE, WHAT WOULD YOU PAINT?
144. IF YOU COULD CHOOSE TO STAY A CERTAIN AGE FOREVER, WHAT AGE WOULD IT BE?
145. IF YOU KNEW THE WORLD WAS ENDING THIS YEAR, WHAT WOULD YOU DO DIFFERENTLY?
146. IF YOU COULD CHOOSE ANYONE, WHO WOULD YOU PICK AS YOUR MENTOR?
147. IF YOU COULD WITNESS ANY EVENT PAST, PRESENT OR FUTURE, WHAT WOULD IT BE?
148. IF YOU COULD LEARN TO DO ANYTHING, WHAT WOULD IT BE?
149. IF YOU HAD TO WORK ON ONLY ONE PROJECT FOR THE NEXT YEAR, WHAT WOULD IT BE?
150. IF YOU WERE IMMORTAL FOR A DAY, WHAT WOULD YOU DO?
151. IF YOU HAD TO CHANGE YOUR FIRST NAME, WHAT WOULD YOU CHANGE IT TO?
152. IF YOU COULD MEET ANYONE, LIVING OR DEAD, WHO WOULD YOU MEET?
153. IF YOU WON THE LOTTERY, WHAT IS THE FIRST THING YOU WOULD DO?

If you would like to get your hands on the templates used inside this book, please go right now to
www.perfectcustomerbook.com/freetemplates

154. IF YOU WERE REINCARNATED AS AN ANIMAL/DRINK/ICE CREAM FLAVOR, WHAT WOULD IT BE?

155. IF YOU COULD KNOW THE ANSWER TO ANY QUESTION, BESIDES "WHAT IS THE MEANING OF LIFE?" WHAT WOULD IT BE?

156. IF YOU COULD BE ANY FICTIONAL CHARACTER, WHO WOULD YOU CHOOSE?

157. WHICH CELEBRITY DO YOU GET MISTAKEN FOR?

158. WHAT DO YOU WANT TO BE WHEN YOU GROW UP?

159. WHEN YOU HAVE 30 MINUTES OF FREE-TIME, HOW DO YOU PASS THE TIME?

160. WHAT WOULD YOU NAME THE AUTOBIOGRAPHY OF YOUR LIFE?

161. WHAT SONGS ARE INCLUDED ON THE SOUNDTRACK TO YOUR LIFE?

162. HAVE YOU EVER HAD SOMETHING HAPPEN TO YOU THAT YOU THOUGHT WAS BAD BUT IT TURNED OUT TO BE FOR THE BEST?

163. WHAT WAS ONE OF THE BEST PARTIES YOU'VE EVER BEEN TO?

164. WHAT WAS THE LAST MOVIE, TV SHOW OR BOOK THAT MADE YOU CRY OR TEAR UP?

165. WHAT'S THE HARDEST THING YOU'VE EVER DONE?

166. WHAT WAS THE LAST EXPERIENCE THAT MADE YOU A STRONGER PERSON?

167. WHAT DID YOU DO GROWING UP THAT GOT YOU INTO TROUBLE?

If you would like to get your hands on the templates used inside this book, please go right now to
www.perfectcustomerbook.com/freetemplates

168. WHEN WAS THE LAST TIME YOU HAD AN AMAZING MEAL?

169. WHAT'S THE BEST/WORST GIFT YOU'VE EVER GIVEN/RECEIVED?

170. WHAT DO YOU MISS MOST ABOUT BEING A KID?

171. WHAT IS YOUR FIRST MEMORY OF BEING REALLY EXCITED?

172. WHAT WAS THE FIRST THING YOU BOUGHT WITH YOUR OWN MONEY?

173. WHEN WAS THE LAST TIME YOU WERE NERVOUS?

174. WHAT IS SOMETHING YOU LEARNED IN THE LAST WEEK?

175. WHAT STORY DOES YOUR FAMILY ALWAYS TELL ABOUT YOU?

176. AT WHAT AGE DID YOU BECOME AN ADULT?

177. IS A PICTURE WORTH A THOUSAND WORDS? ELABORATE.

178. WHERE'S WALDO?

179. THE BEST PART OF WAKING UP IS?

180. HOW NOW BROWN COW?

181. WHASSSSSUUUUPPPPPP?

182. HOW DO YOU DEFINE HONESTY?

183. WHAT IS YOUR BIGGEST FEAR OR WORRY?

184. WHAT IS THE MAIN THING THAT MAKES YOU UNIQUE?

185. IF YOU HAD TO EVACUATE YOUR HOUSE IMMEDIATELY, WHAT IS THE ONE THING YOU WOULD GRAB ON THE WAY OUT?

186. WHAT FACIAL EXPRESSION OR MOVEMENT DO YOU DO WHEN YOU ARE LYING?

If you would like to get your hands on the templates used inside this book, please go right now to
www.perfectcustomerbook.com/freetemplates

187. WHAT IS THE OLDEST ITEM YOU OWN?

188. IF SOMEONE WAS TO GIVE YOU ONE GIFT, MONEY IS NO OBJECT, WHAT WOULD YOU WANT TO RECEIVE?

189. WHAT DOES IT MEAN TO HAVE COURAGE?

190. DO YOU LIKE YOUR NAME?

191. DO YOU HAVE A NICKNAME? WHAT IS IT?

192. IF YOU COULD HAVE ANY SPECIAL MAGIC, WHAT WOULD IT BE?

193. IF YOU HAD THREE WISHES, WHAT WOULD YOU WISH?

194. WHAT IS YOUR GREATEST STRENGTH?

195. WHAT IS YOUR WORST WEAKNESS?

196. IF YOU COULD PREDICT THE FUTURE, WHAT WOULD YOU DO WITH THAT KNOWLEDGE?

197. IS YOUR FAVORITE TIME THE PAST, PRESENT OR THE FUTURE?

198. WHERE DO YOU SEE YOURSELF IN 20 YEARS?

199. WHO IS THE ONE PERSON THAT HELPED TO MAKE YOU WHO YOU ARE TODAY?

200. IF YOU WERE PUNISHED FOR A CRIME, WHAT TYPE OF PUNISHMENT WOULD YOU CHOOSE?

201. DESCRIBE A TIME YOU GOT INTO TROUBLE.

202. WHAT DO YOU DO WHEN YOU FIRST WAKE UP IN THE MORNING?

203. WHAT MAKES YOU A GOOD PERSON?

204. WHAT WOULD YOUR OBITUARY SAY?

205. WHAT IS YOUR GREATEST REGRET?

206. HOW WOULD YOU DESCRIBE STANDING ON A BEACH LOOKING AT THE OCEAN?

If you would like to get your hands on the templates used inside this book, please go right now to
www.perfectcustomerbook.com/freetemplates

207. WHAT IS YOUR FAVORITE OUTFIT TO WEAR?
208. WHAT DO YOU DO WHEN YOU ARE DRIVING ALONE IN A CAR?
209. IF A FRIEND IS BEING BULLIED OR HARASSED BY SOMEONE, WHAT DO YOU DO?
210. REFLECT ON THE CHARACTERISTICS OF YOUR BEST FRIEND. WHAT MAKES HIM OR HER SO SPECIAL?
211. HAS ANYONE CLOSE TO YOU PASSED AWAY?
212. DESCRIBE A TIME YOU FELL IN LOVE.
213. CAN YOU KEEP SECRETS? DESCRIBE A TIME YOU DIDN'T.
214. HOW DO YOU SHOW YOUR LOVE FOR OTHERS?
215. WHAT IS THE NICEST THING ANYONE HAS EVER DONE FOR YOU?
216. IF YOU COULD BECOME ANYONE'S FRIEND THAT YOU WANT, WHO WOULD YOU CHOOSE?
217. ARE YOU THE TYPE OF PERSON WITH LOTS OF FRIENDS OR JUST A FEW CLOSE ONES?
218. WHAT IS ONE QUALITY YOU ADMIRE MOST IN OTHERS?
219. DO YOU PREFER TO BE WITH THOSE WHO ARE YOUNGER OR OLDER THAN YOU ARE?
220. IF YOU COULD ASK ME ONE QUESTION, AND I HAD TO ANSWER YOU TRUTHFULLY, WHAT WOULD YOU WANT TO KNOW?
221. WHAT IS THE MEANEST THING YOU HAVE EVER DONE TO SOMEONE?
222. WHO IS ONE FRIEND FROM YOUR PAST YOU WANT TO RECONNECT WITH?

If you would like to get your hands on the templates used inside this book, please go right now to
www.perfectcustomerbook.com/freetemplates

223. WHEN DID YOU KISS FOR THE FIRST TIME AND WHAT WAS IT LIKE?

224. DESCRIBE AN ACTIVITY THAT YOU THINK IS TRULY ROMANTIC.

225. IF YOU WERE TO WRITE A LOVE NOTE TO YOUR SWEETHEART, WHAT WOULD IT SAY?

226. WHEN YOU ARE IN TROUBLE, WHOM DO YOU CALL FOR HELP?

227. WHO ARE THE PEOPLE YOU LOVE THE MOST?

228. IF YOU COULD SPEAK ANY LANGUAGE, WHAT WOULD IT BE AND WHY?

229. IF YOU HAD TO PICK ONE PLACE IN YOUR TOWN TO BRING A TOURIST, WHERE WOULD YOU GO?

230. WHAT IS THE ONE CAUSE THAT YOU FEEL MOST PASSIONATE ABOUT?

231. IF YOU LIVED IN THE PIONEER DAYS, WOULD YOU HAVE TRAVELED WEST OR STAYED PUT IN THE EAST?

232. WHICH IS YOUR FAVORITE NON-PROFIT ORGANIZATION? WHAT DO YOU DO TO HELP THEM?

233. IF YOU COULD TRAVEL TO SPACE, WOULD YOU GO?

234. IF YOU COULD MOVE ANYWHERE, WHERE WOULD YOU GO AND WHY?

235. WOULD YOU WANT TO TRAVEL THE WORLD ON A BOAT IN THE SEA?

236. WHEN YOU TRAVEL AWAY FROM HOME, DO YOU MISS IT?

If you would like to get your hands on the templates used inside this book, please go right now to
www.perfectcustomerbook.com/freetemplates

237. WHAT IS THE GREATEST CRISIS WE FACE AS A WORLD?
238. DESCRIBE YOUR FAVORITE VACATION.
239. IF YOU COULD WRITE YOUR OWN BILL OF RIGHTS, WHAT WOULD YOU INCLUDE?
240. WHAT IS GOING ON TODAY IN THE WORLD THAT AFFECTS YOU THE MOST?
241. WHAT BAD HABIT WOULD YOU BE WILLING TO GIVE UP IF IT GUARANTEED YOU WOULD LIVE TO BE 100?
242. WHAT IS YOUR FAVORITE THING TO EAT?
243. WHAT IS ONE FOOD THAT YOU WILL NOT EAT?
244. WHAT IS YOUR FAVORITE WAY TO EXERCISE?
245. IF YOU HAD TO CHOOSE TO BE BLIND OR DEAF, WHICH ONE WOULD YOU PICK?
246. HAVE YOU EVER BEEN TO A HOSPITAL? WHY?
247. IF YOU COULD HAVE SOMEONE ELSE'S FACE, WHOM WOULD YOU CHOOSE?
248. DESCRIBE A VIVID DREAM YOU HAVE HAD.
249. WHAT PHYSICAL FEATURE DO YOU LEAST LIKE ABOUT YOURSELF?
250. WOULD YOU WANT TO KNOW THE EXACT DAY OF YOUR DEATH?
251. IF YOU HAD TO PICK ONE HERO, WHO WOULD IT BE?
252. IF YOU COULD PICK ONE THING TO CHANGE ABOUT YOUR SCHOOL OR JOB, WHAT WOULD IT BE?
253. WHAT ARE MOST PROUD OF?

If you would like to get your hands on the templates used inside this book, please go right now to
www.perfectcustomerbook.com/freetemplates

254. ARE YOU THE KIND OF PERSON WHO WANTS TO BE THE BIG FISH IN A LITTLE POND OR THE LITTLE FISH IN THE BIG POND?

255. DESCRIBE A TIME WHEN YOU WANTED TO QUIT, BUT DIDN'T.

256. MENTION ONE GOAL. WHEN YOU HOPE TO ACCOMPLISH IT?

257. IS COMPETITION GOOD FOR YOU?

258. IF YOU COULD STUDY ANYTHING YOU WANTED IN SCHOOL, WHAT WOULD YOU WANT TO LEARN MORE ABOUT?

259. WHAT IS SOMETHING YOU LEARNED IN SCHOOL THAT YOU THINK IS USELESS TO YOU TODAY?

260. WHEN SOMEONE FAILS AT SOMETHING, WHAT SHOULD HE OR SHE DO?

261. IF YOU COULD PICK ANY CAREER, WHAT WOULD YOU WANT TO BE?

262. DO YOU WANT TO BE FAMOUS?
ENTERTAINMENT QUESTIONS

263. IF YOU COULD BECOME A CHARACTER IN A TV SHOW OR MOVIE, WHO WOULD YOU CHOSE TO BE?

264. WHAT IS YOUR FAVORITE OUTSIDE ACTIVITY?

265. WHAT IS YOUR FAVORITE HOLIDAY AND HOW DO YOU CELEBRATE IT?

266. WHAT IS YOUR FAVORITE SPORT? DO YOU PLAY OR JUST WATCH?

267. HAVE YOU BEEN ON A ROLLER COASTER? WHAT DID IT FEEL LIKE?

If you would like to get your hands on the templates used inside this book, please go right now to
www.perfectcustomerbook.com/freetemplates

268. IF YOU HAD TO SPEND A DAY NOT USING ANY TECHNOLOGY, WHAT WOULD YOU DO?
269. DESCRIBE THE PERFECT PARTY.
270. WHAT IS YOUR FAVORITE TYPE OF ART?
271. WHAT SPORT DO YOU THINK YOU ARE THE BEST AT?
272. DO YOU PLAY AN INSTRUMENT?
273. WHICH IS YOUR FAVORITE SONG?
274. IF YOU COULD BE A CARTOON CHARACTER, WHO WOULD YOU WANT TO BE?
275. DO YOU KNOW ANY JOKES? IF SO, TELL ME ONE.
276. WHAT IS THE ONE THING THAT MAKES YOU LAUGH THE HARDEST?
277. WHAT MAKES YOUR FAMILY UNIQUE FROM OTHERS?
278. WHEN YOU THINK BACK TO YOUR CHILDHOOD, WHAT WAS THE HARDEST PART ABOUT BEING A KID?
279. WHAT ARE SOME OF YOUR FAMILY'S TRADITIONS?
280. DO YOU KNOW HOW YOU GOT YOUR NAME?
281. ARE YOU LIKE YOUR PARENTS OR DIFFERENT? HOW?

Now it's time to give your perfect customer avatar a name and a face.

If you would like to get your hands on the templates used inside this book, please go right now to
www.perfectcustomerbook.com/freetemplates

What does he look like?

It might sound kind of funny to you, but this is the person you'll be talking to when creating content and other marketing materials.

Giving him a name and a face will make it easier to actually talk to your perfect customer. Browse through stock images and see if you can find a picture to associate with him.

Create a short "life story" for your customer avatar. Explain how he has come to need your help.

If you would like to get your hands on the templates used inside this book, please go right now to
www.perfectcustomerbook.com/freetemplates

EXAMPLE: <u>Customer Avatar "Tom" Example</u>

Step #1:

- Tom is 21, a general laborer in Toronto, Ontario Canada currently dry walling new commercial units while living in an old camping trailer he pulls behind his 1994 Volvo 960 GLE station wagon.
- Tom is single
- Tom has no children
- Tom's monthly expenses are $1200 not including his food
- Tom's monthly income is $2800
- Tom has a product but has no idea how to make a website to sell it
- Tom wants a website that he can write articles on and sell his info-products on dry walling for novices and similar construction related info-products.

If you would like to get your hands on the templates used inside this book, please go right now to
www.perfectcustomerbook.com/freetemplates

- Tom is very motivated and takes pride in his work. He always finishes what he starts.
- He takes the best out of everything and adapts it to suit his current purpose.
- Tom mostly listens to country music and his current favorite song is:
- Tom likes to go to the bar to unwind, he enjoys watching various sports on the TVs at the bar and drinking 3-4 beers.
- Tom doesn't own a TV in his camper but enjoys watching episodes of *Supernatural* and *Boardwalk Empire*.
- Tom reads a lot of how-to guides (mostly on how to build things around the house and how to repair and fix things around the home as well as gardening books)
- Tom wants to buy a house so he can have his own space, also so he can have a garden and start a family home.
- Tom likes to read science magazines
- Tom likes to keep a short scruffy beard and showers daily after work and often uses his favorite Stetson cologne.
- Tom doesn't mind learning but wants something he can figure out quickly
- Tom's friends enjoy his company and find him dedicated and quick witted, they think his decision to enter internet marketing is intriguing and more difficult than he thinks.

If you would like to get your hands on the templates used inside this book, please go right now to
www.perfectcustomerbook.com/freetemplates

- Tom loves to prove people wrong and hates being told he can't do something
- When Tom decides to do something he gives it 110%
- Toms biggest desire is to own his own home mortgage free so he can find a woman to marry and have kids, he wants to quit his job so he has his free time to create products whenever he feels he can help his community, he wants to promote other people's products that he believes in using marketing techniques he intends to learn so he can make money without doing any hard work so he has time for his garden and his future girlfriend.
- He wants to have his own place before he finds someone to settle down with, he dates occasionally but nothing serious.
- Currently Tom is trying to find a method to start with so he can sell his current eBook about mudding and dry walling for novices.
- Tom wants to feel like he can be as creative with his online projects as he is with his construction work.
- Tom's biggest fear is not understanding how to use or update his website as time goes on and updates come out for plugins etc.
- Tom wants to learn more about web design and web programming but wants something

If you would like to get your hands on the templates used inside this book, please go right now to
www.perfectcustomerbook.com/freetemplates

he can use right away to sell his eBook course.

- Tom's biggest frustration is not having enough time to learn because of his work schedule, and not knowing which option to use because there are so many to choose from.

Step #2:

Listing all the Benefits & Features of either your product, or a product you're promoting or a service or services that you're offering if you get stuck understanding any step you can look at the EXAMPLE files I provided to get a feel for how this all fits together.

If you would like to get your hands on the templates used inside this book, please go right now to www.perfectcustomerbook.com/freetemplates

Product/Service Name:	
Product/Service Description:	
Product/Service Price:	

MAIN FEATURES	MAIN BENEFITS

SECONDARY FEATURES	SECONDARY BENEFITS

If you would like to get your hands on the templates used inside this book, please go right now to
www.perfectcustomerbook.com/freetemplates

<table>
<tr><td></td><td></td></tr>
</table>

Example: **Features & Benefits EXAMPLE for Tom**

Product/Service Name:	Dave's Web Development
Product/Service Description:	Custom websites complete with payment gateways and additional premium plugins for internet marketing of products and services. *Hosting & Domain Name Required (although I will provide any help necessary in getting that and understanding how to use it) Extremely Affordable, Professional Designs while maintaining a highly functional experience. From Start to Finish in as little time as possible. Comes with the following Premium WordPress Plugins: Authority Pro 3, GPlus Activator, Social RankJet, WP Target Buddy WP Traffic Recycler, WP News Flash. Premium Theme Extra @ $50
Product/Service Price:	$450.00 with a $100 First Time Customer Rebate (Domain and Hosting Costs Separate) + $50 Extra for Premium WordPress Theme.

MAIN FEATURES	MAIN BENEFITS
• CUSTOM, UNIQUE DESIGN, PROFESSIONAL • 6 PREMIUM WORDPRESS PLUGINS THAT TRANSFORM YOUR WEBSITE INTO A FULLY FUNCTIONAL INTERNET MARKETING PLATFORM FOR YOUR PRODUCTS OR SERVICES COMPLETE WITH PAYMENT GATEWAYS • NEWBIE FRIENDLY, SEO FRIENDLY	• Affordable enough for the average working person • The plugins cover the current standard for Internet Marketing, providing a platform for maximizing your reach and profits that isn't outdated • Easy to get started even if you have a PLR Product or doing affiliate marketing

If you would like to get your hands on the templates used inside this book, please go right now to
www.perfectcustomerbook.com/freetemplates

• QUICK TURNAROUND	• You stand out as unique because it isn't just a copy and paste setup
• HELP WITH MARKETING	• Current Marketing Help means getting in the game fast with the best head start
• LOW PRICE WITH AFFORDABLE EXTRAS / ADD-ONS	
SECONDARY FEATURES	**SECONDARY BENEFITS**
• ALL PREMIUM PLUGINS COME PRE-CONFIGURED WITH INFORMATION PROVIDED BY CLIENT	• No Confusing Plugin Setup means they can focus on using the system and making sales/marketing and not trying to get the system to work. Functional "Right Out of the Box"
• LINKS TO TRAINING VIDEOS FOR ALL PLUGINS	• Links to training videos means they can learn as they go, or give the training videos to their outsourced help
• 7 DAYS OF ASSISTANCE AFTER FINAL SETUP IF ANY OF THE TUTORIALS ARE CONFUSING OR SOMETHING ISN'T WORKING	• Peace of Mind knowing they have 7 days of personal help with any issues
• ABILITY TO CREATE AN ENTIRE SALES FUNNEL, INCLUDING OPT-IN / SQUEEZE PAGES, VIDEO SALES PAGES, STANDARD SALES PAGES, LEGAL PAGES, PRE-LAUNCH PAGES, UPSELL PAGES, EXIT SQUEEZE PAGES, BUYER OPT-IN PAGES, THANK YOU / DOWNLOAD PAGES, DMCA POLICY PAGES, TERMS OF USE PAGES AND MUCH MUCH MORE	• Setup with their Favorite Payment Processor means they can start making money right away
	• Having the ability to Sell Unlimited Products or Services means having the flexibility to Sell more and change settings and pages as you go so they aren't stuck with a static website; Flexibility

If you would like to get your hands on the templates used inside this book, please go right now to
www.perfectcustomerbook.com/freetemplates

Step #3: Fill Out Your Avatar's Timeline Sheet in Relation to Your Product / Service

Avatar Name	
Product/Service Name	

Timeline	Help (typically the benefits)	Appeal (typically the features)
Will (Typically the benefits		
Could (Typically the benefits		
Has (features of benefits or typically for creating back-story type marketing & testimonials or repeat customers.		

If you would like to get your hands on the templates used inside this book, please go right now to
www.perfectcustomerbook.com/freetemplates

Tom's Timeline EXAMPLE (Will, Could, Has)

vatar Name:	Tom Woodson	
roduct/Service ame:	Dave's Web Development (1) Website [New Customer]	
Timeline	Help (Typically the Benefits)	Appeal (Typically the Features)
Will (Typically the Benefits)	• Having Current And Updated Premium Plugins (Since Tom's new to IM he doesn't know yet how they will help him) • Being Ready to Use Quickly • Having the Extra Marketing Help (Because Tom Already Has A Product He Wants to Sell • Having Everything Come Pre-Configured (Plugins Etc.)	• Being Ready to Use Quickly • That He Can Promote Multiple Things in the Future • Having A Custom Theme (Tom likes to Stand Out And Will Appreciate Having A Professional Theme to Work With And Price is Not Necessarily An Issue for Tom) • Having the Extra Marketing Help (Because Tom Already Has A Product He Wants to Sell

If you would like to get your hands on the templates used inside this book, please go right now to
www.perfectcustomerbook.com/freetemplates

	• Getting Access to the Training for Each Plugin so He Can Learn to Do Things On His Own (Tom is a "Hands On" Type of Personality) • Having it Integrated With His PayPal Account	• Having Everything Come Pre-Configured (Plugins etc.) • Having 7 Extra Days of Personal Support • Getting Access to the Training for Each Plugin so He Can Learn to Do Things On His Own (Tom is a "Hands On" Type of Personality) • Having it Integrated With His PayPal Account
<u>Could</u> (Typically the Benefits)	• Being SEO Friendly "Out of the Box" (Because Tom Might Not Spend A Lot of Time Worrying About That Right Away Since He's New He Already Has A Lot to Learn • Being Newbie Friendly (Tom is New But He's A Smart Guy And Figures Things Out By Himself Very Quickly) He's Good At Finding the Necessary Tutorials And Lessons on YouTube or elsewhere but he will enjoy how easy it is to use "Out of the Box"	• Inexpensive (Tom can easily afford it so it wouldn't necessarily be a make or break situation) • Being Newbie Friendly (Tom is New But He's A Smart Guy And Figures Things Out By Himself Very Quickly) He's Good At Finding the Necessary Tutorials And Lessons on YouTube or elsewhere but he will enjoy how easy it is to use "Out of the Box" • Being SEO Friendly "Out of the Box" (Because Tom Might Not Spend A Lot of Time Worrying About

	• Having 7 Extra Days of Personal Support (In Case Tom feels Like He May Be Overwhelmed With All The New Information)	That Right Away Since He's New He Already Has A Lot to Learn • Having 7 Extra Days of Personal Support (In Case Tom feels Like He May Be Overwhelmed With All The New Information)
Has (Typically for Creating Backstory Type Marketing & Testimonials or Repeat Customers)	NOT APPLICABLE FOR THIS PARTICULAR VERSION OF TOM	NOT APPLICABLE FOR THIS PARTICULAR VERSION OF TOM

If you would like to get your hands on the templates used inside this book, please go right now to
www.perfectcustomerbook.com/freetemplates

Step 4) Fill Out Needs/Wants/Likes Chart

Needs	Wants	Likes

If you would like to get your hands on the templates used inside this
book, please go right now to
www.perfectcustomerbook.com/freetemplates

EXAMPLE: Needs, Wants, Likes EXAMPLE for Tom

Needs	Wants	Likes
• Long-term Solution	• Fast Overall Turnaround	• Pre-Setup Plugins
• To Be Able to See Results	• To Be Able To Buy His Own Home	• Getting Help to Get Started Faster
• Validation This Can Replace His Current Income Fast & Consistently	• To Be Able To Get Paid Quickly	• The Freedom From the "9 to 5" Type of Job
• To Feel Creative & "in Control" Quickly	• The Ability to Change the Sites Appearance in the Future	• The Excitement of Learning Something New
• A Complete Solution	• To Feel Confident He Can Manage Everything in the Future	• Amount of Free Help He's Already Found On Using Everything Included in the Package
• Extra Help to Understand Everything	• The Site & Plugins to Be Current & Updated	
• It Fully Functional When Completed, Payment Gateway Tested	• Tutorials For Every Plugin & Process Involved in Running the Site & Making Money	• Tutorials So He Can Learn How to Make His Own Changes
• Ability to Charge Appropriate Taxes	• Current & Updated Plugins and Platform	• Multiple Payment Processors Already Built in and Ready to Go
• Extra Marketing Help	• A Few Marketing Options (Not Just One)	• Premium Theme Option
• PayPal Payment Gateway	• To Start with Easy Methods	• Premium Plugins
• Legal Pages	• To Know Where to Learn on His Own	• Being Taught and Not Dictated to
• Turnkey Solution		• Cost Efficient Solutions but Also Wants to Know the More Costly Methods too
• Long-term Solution For Promoting His Products		

If you would like to get your hands on the templates used inside this book, please go right now to
www.perfectcustomerbook.com/freetemplates

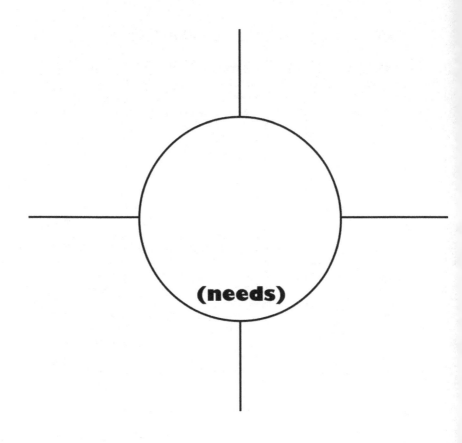

(needs)

If you would like to get your hands on the templates used inside this book, please go right now to
www.perfectcustomerbook.com/freetemplates

Examples:

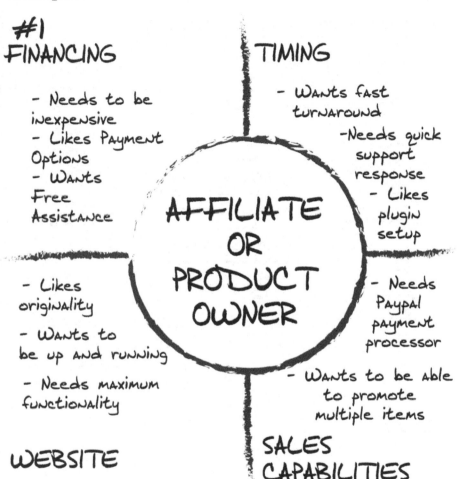

#1
FINANCING

- Needs to be inexpensive
- Likes Payment Options
- Wants Free Assistance

TIMING

- Wants fast turnaround
- Needs quick support response
- Likes plugin setup

AFFILIATE OR PRODUCT OWNER

- Likes originality
- Wants to be up and running
- Needs maximum functionality

- Needs Paypal payment processor
- Wants to be able to promote multiple items

WEBSITE

SALES CAPABILITIES

If you would like to get your hands on the templates used inside this book, please go right now to
www.perfectcustomerbook.com/freetemplates

#2

PRICE

- Needs no expensive workout equipment
- Likes no expensive food to buy
- Wants to get his/her moneys worth

TIMING

- Needs quick lessons
- Likes weight loss claims 30 days - 20 lbs
- Wants fast consistant results

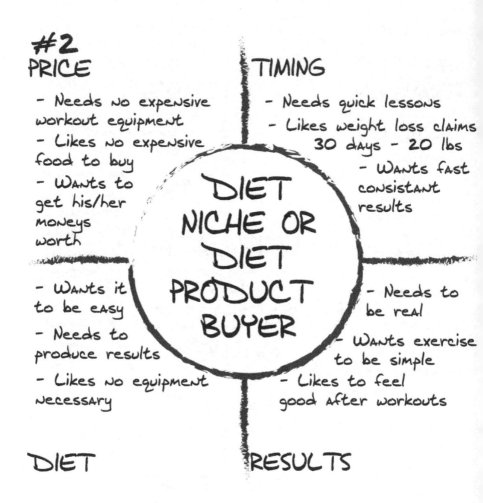

DIET NICHE OR DIET PRODUCT BUYER

- Wants it to be easy
- Needs to produce results
- Likes no equipment necessary

- Needs to be real
- Wants exercise to be simple
- Likes to feel good after workouts

DIET

RESULTS

#3

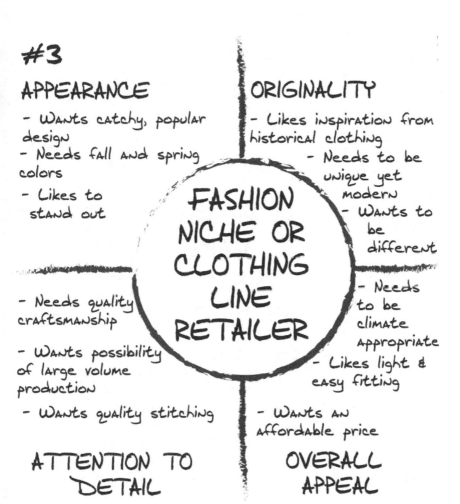

APPEARANCE
- Wants catchy, popular design
- Needs fall and spring colors
- Likes to stand out

ORIGINALITY
- Likes inspiration from historical clothing
- Needs to be unique yet modern
- Wants to be different

FASHION NICHE OR CLOTHING LINE RETAILER

- Needs quality craftsmanship
- Wants possibility of large volume production
- Wants quality stitching

- Needs to be climate appropriate
- Likes light & easy fitting
- Wants an affordable price

ATTENTION TO DETAIL

OVERALL APPEAL

If you would like to get your hands on the templates used inside this book, please go right now to
www.perfectcustomerbook.com/freetemplates

#4

SIMPLICITY

- Wants least amount of steps necessary to achieve results
- Likes step by step training
- Training process needs to be simple

- Wants money within 3 days of learning method
- Likes quick step by step instructions
- Needs to learn fast

TIMING

RESULTS

- Wants consistant income
- Likes a method that won't become saturated
- Needs to see money within 3 days

IM NICHE OR MAKE MONEY PRODUCT BUYER

- Wants minimal risk of loss
- Needs to make income with minimal investment
- Likes multiple ways to monetize each possible action

COST PER ACTION

If you would like to get your hands on the templates used inside this book, please go right now to
www.perfectcustomerbook.com/freetemplates

This is designed to give you an idea of how the categories can change based on what you're creating your "customer avatar" for.

The center of the "needs wheel" is the hub where you can list the common needs of your customer avatar. Sometimes you won't have any common needs, in which case you can identify what a few of their strongest needs are so you can focus those into your marketing campaigns. (In the example above I have left the center empty but you can look at my example below for Tom to see a finished example.)

Now typically I usually do this all on paper because I have more room to write and I can make my "Needs Wheel" a lot larger, I've also tried printing off 3-4 "Needs Wheels" and filling out a few of them because when I do this in my marketing I end up with a lot more information than I've provided in my examples and I hope you do too, this is just to give you an idea of how to put this all together so you get the most out of your "Customer Avatar"

Below is a graphical representation of how I determine which needs are most crucial for my "customer avatar" example, Tom

If you would like to get your hands on the templates used inside this book, please go right now to
www.perfectcustomerbook.com/freetemplates

My Customer Avatar EXAMPLE Tom

TIMING

- Needs "turn key" solution
- Likes pre set up plug-ins
- Wants fast overall turnaround
- Likes getting help to get started faster
- Wants to be able to buy his own home
- Likes the freedom from the 9-5 type job
- Wants to get paid quickly
- Needs a long term solution
- Needs to be able to see results.

SALES CAPABILITIES

- Likes multiple payment processors already built in
- Needs ability to charge appropriate taxes
- Wanst tutorials for every plug-in and process involved.
- Likes premium theme option
- Needs extra marketing help
- Wants site to be highly customizable.
- Needs paypal gateway
- Needs legal pages
- Likes premium plug-ins
- Needs longterm solution for promoting product

NEEDS

- Long Term Solution
- Turnkey Solution
- A Complete Solution
- Longterm solution for promoting his products
* To know how everythign works together
* Extra Marketing Help
* A Good Basis to Star and a Solid Direction to move in.
* Validation that this can replace his current income fast and consistently.
** To feel creative and in control
** To be able to see results
** Fully functional when complete, payment gateway tested

WEBSITE

- Needs a complete solution
- Wants the ability to change sites appearance in future.
- Wants to feel confident
- He can manage everything in the future.
- Likes the excitement of learning something new.
- Needs extra help to understand everything.
- Wants site to be unique
- Wants site to be fully functional when completed payment gateway tested

EXTRA MARKETING HELP

- Wants a few marketing options
- Wants to start with easy methods
- Needs to see results quickly and consistently
- Likes being taught and not dictated to.
- Wants to know where to learn on his own
- Needs a good basis and a solid direction to move in
- Likes cost efficient solutions but wants to know more costly methods too
- Needs to know how everything works together.

If you would like to get your hands on the templates used inside this book, please go right now to
www.perfectcustomerbook.com/freetemplates

Step #6: "Putting It All Together"

This is where all of the information we've put together on the needs wheel will help us write our marketing pieces, taking into account all of their needs, likes and wants as well and since we filled out "Your Avatar's Timeline (Will, Could, Have)" we'll have a bit of their timeline taken into account. The rest of their timeline will be basic things like "when do they expect to see results", or "how long does it take to learn/implement", to "how long will it take to complete", or "how long until they can buy a new car or home" etc. getting into the more personal side of their life.

One of the reasons for separating the similar needs is so you can pick pairs of needs to use in the following method:

Using my adaptation of nested loops; (a method of telling a story without coming to the conclusion before starting another story, and on and on until you come back and finish telling the first story, then finishing the second story etc..) Using the needs, wants & likes you've created, write the basis of a story from beginning to end explaining your customer avatars experience in life with your

If you would like to get your hands on the templates used inside this book, please go right now to
www.perfectcustomerbook.com/freetemplates

product using the following layout. Then go back and tweak it all and make it flow logically, getting the basis of the story from beginning to end makes it easier to edit. Also, it might help thinking about starting with the end and working your way to the beginning, because in essence you want your potential customers to take an action of some kind, so start with that action and by using your customer avatar, you climb your way back to the beginning of how your customer avatar got to the end goal (buying your product).

Customer Avatar Looking for Solution of Some Kind > Customer Avatar Finding Your Solution > How / Why Customer Avatar Decided to Buy Product / Service > Customer Avatar Buys Product > Customer Avatar Gets X, Y, Z Results from Product / Service.

This is just one method but it should get you thinking in the right direction.

Start off your copy/story talking about need (a) and how your product or service uniquely fulfills that need (a) while talking about how they can get one of their wants (a) fulfilled in a way they like (a) (that also fulfills one of their likes (a)) then finish that sentence or section with need (b)

If you would like to get your hands on the templates used inside this book, please go right now to
www.perfectcustomerbook.com/freetemplates

Then in the next section of your sales letter or marketing piece start talking about need (c) followed by how they can get one of their wants (b) fulfilled in a way they like (b) (that also fulfills one of their likes (b)) then finish that sentence or section with need (d)

You can do this as many times as necessary to complete your sales letter but eventually you'll need to come back and "close" the loops you've opened (the stories you began telling but didn't quite finish) and you'll do this in a similar fashion:

You want to "close" the loops in the same order that you "opened" them in.

So you'll want to finish the first story [need (a)] while talking about the same or similar wants (a) and likes (a) in a story type of manner] and then also "close" the final need (b) while transitioning into "closing" the second/next loop [need (c) also while talking about the same or similar wants (b) and likes (b) in a story type of manner] and then also again close the final need (d).

I'll give a very basic and apparent example so you get a good understanding of what I'm talking about here and I'll also do my best to explain it in the video for this section.

If you would like to get your hands on the templates used inside this book, please go right now to
www.perfectcustomerbook.com/freetemplates

Example: (I won't be utilizing the open loop / close loop in this example)

Using my "Customer Avatar" Tom, I could say.

Tom immediately felt confident he'd be able to manage his turnkey website in the future when updates were needed because the tutorials came ready for his iPhone 5s so he could learn everything he needed at his own pace while he ate his lunch at work and on breaks. He'd be able to update everything and make all the changes he wants in the future after he learns how while his product is already setup and making sales with premium fully functional marketing plugins, everything Tom needs now and in the future to sell his info products or any other affiliate offer.

At night Tom makes small changes to his marketing and sales pages with the tips he's been getting to see if it improves conversions, after he checks his PayPal account to see the day's earnings while listening to *"That's My Kind Of Night"* by Luke Bryan. Tom feels really confident about the future. With the extra help he's been getting, he's already started to see a few sales and now he's thinking of setting up another one of the payment processors. He's starting to really think this could replace his "9

If you would like to get your hands on the templates used inside this book, please go right now to
www.perfectcustomerbook.com/freetemplates

to 5" job in a couple of months at this rate, maybe even faster.

The creativity with this really lies with you, but creating a story using nest loops will have to be another product because it'll take the emphasis off of creating your "customer avatar" which is important to get good at first, then this should be more than enough to get you started, and I'm sure you'll see how this can make all the difference in your marketing when you get really good at it.

There are tons of ways you can use the information from your customer avatar and the needs wheel to spruce up your marketing. If you do any copywriting, it will definitely be one of the most used weapons in your arsenal.

This is a powerful way of using "nested loops" in your marketing, although the real magic comes from your ability to "begin" talking about how your product/service will fulfill their needs using stories that you don't quite finish telling.

Has anyone ever told you a story and they get distracted half way through and start talking about something sort of related? And then all of a sudden after talking about that they remember what they were initially talking about and then finish the

If you would like to get your hands on the templates used inside this book, please go right now to
www.perfectcustomerbook.com/freetemplates

original story? And you're left thinking, "Oh yeah! I forgot about that..." well this is a powerful way of imbedding things into the unconscious and in this case, imbedding the concepts and ideas that your product or service can fulfill their needs, likes and wants.

It might be hard coming up with a set of stories to use to sell your product or services initially, especially if you haven't answered many of the Customer Avatar Questions and this is where those "extra" questions can come in handy because it can give you extra things to talk about in relation to your customer avatar his/her hobbies and his/her life experience so as an example phrase, if you were targeting the lazy surfer type, you could tell your "customer avatar" a story about how he could realistically surf more often and do less work or add another layer to it and tell your "customer avatar" a story about how a lazy surfer friend of yours was able to surf more often and do most of his work from the beach tethering internet from his phone.

So as you can see it can really help if you give your "customer avatar" as much of a background as you can. It's really important that this background comes from actual market research in your niche and this really isn't too hard; find a forum in your

If you would like to get your hands on the templates used inside this book, please go right now to
www.perfectcustomerbook.com/freetemplates

niche, or a popular blog, and search Facebook. Facebook is a goldmine for market research, find some groups in your niche and check out the people in the group. You can get a lot of information this way. Don't forget to just search for popular keywords in your niche too. Facebook search has really expanded quite a bit and you might not have noticed any changes until you check it out ☺

The idea here is to tell stories and "tall tales" starring your "customer avatar" in a way that relates to your product / service's benefits and features.

You can also use this to create a mascot avatar or spokesperson for your company or business sort of like an Uncle Ben's, Ronald McDonald, Aunt Jemima, Flo (Progressive Insurance) and you can use this individual to sell to your "customer avatar." Creating layers of avatars that can communicate together makes your marketing sound a lot less like your customers are being "talked at" and instead they feel like they are part of the conversation, or at least like they're eavesdropping in on the conversation and not being "sold to." Instead it comes across a lot less aggressive, especially if you're selling something with a higher price ticket. Done right you could even act out two avatars in a

If you would like to get your hands on the templates used inside this book, please go right now to
www.perfectcustomerbook.com/freetemplates

sales video writing a clever script using everything you have at your disposal, just like "acting" in your own commercial instead of "being yourself" which some people find intimidating, but if that's not you then I'm sure you wouldn't mind trying something new anyway because you're already confident on camera.

With cold calling you can create customer avatars of tricky or stubborn personalities you come across and by creating a more elaborate customer avatar you can find ways of inoculating against their objections before they even get to voice them.

It can even help writing headlines or short text ad spaces because you'll be able to literally target your age demographics, gender, income level, and interests. And by doing this, you'll avoid spending a lot of money on the broad sweep. Instead, laser target your focus on demographics that match your customer avatar and in turn your marketing/sales pages and videos will get exactly the customers that you want, which will also cut down on your refund rates.

If you would like to get your hands on the templates used inside this book, please go right now to
www.perfectcustomerbook.com/freetemplates

CLOSING Thoughts.

So in closing I hope you really give this an honest effort because I guarantee that it CAN and WILL make all the difference in your marketing. There's a good reason why the largest companies and corporations spend so much money creating their customer avatar. It's vital market research, if you're serious about developing your craft.

If your brand targets several submarkets, create an avatar for each of these.

Many businesses have more than one customer segment they will want to reach. Create a customer avatar for each of these.

If you would like to get your hands on the templates used inside this book, please go right now to
www.perfectcustomerbook.com/freetemplates

Use your perfect customer avatar to connect with your target market and watch your conversions and sales skyrocket.

Now that you have tapped into your perfect customer's psychology, look at life through their eyes. Do you feel their excitement? Can you understand their pain?

Put yourself in their shoes every time you create content, ad copy, or marketing material. Use his language to mirror his words in a natural, authentic way. If you are able to master the art of feeling and thinking exactly as your perfect customer does, you will be able to create marketing campaigns that resonates with them.

They will feel as if you know what they are thinking. They will feel completely understood; as if they are at home.

If you would like to get your hands on the templates used inside this book, please go right now to
www.perfectcustomerbook.com/freetemplates

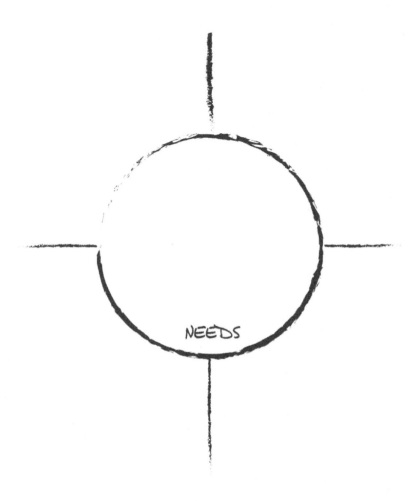

NEEDS

If you would like to get your hands on the templates used inside this book, please go right now to
www.perfectcustomerbook.com/freetemplates

Product/Service Name:	
Product/Service Description:	
Product/Service Price:	

MAIN FEATURES	MAIN BENEFITS

SECONDARY FEATURES	SECONDARY BENEFITS

If you would like to get your hands on the templates used inside this book, please go right now to
www.perfectcustomerbook.com/freetemplates

Avatar Name		
Product/Service Name		
Timeline	Help (typically the benefits)	Appeal (typically the features)
Will (Typically the benefits		
Could (Typically the benefits		
Has (features of benefits or typically for creating back-story type marketing & testimonials or repeat customers.		

If you would like to get your hands on the templates used inside this
book, please go right now to
www.perfectcustomerbook.com/freetemplates

Needs	Wants	Likes

If you would like to get your hands on the templates used inside this book, please go right now to
www.perfectcustomerbook.com/freetemplates

Matt Bacak is considered by many to be an Internet Marketing Legend. Using his stealth marketing techniques, he became a best-selling author with a huge fan base of over 300k people in his niche and built several multi-million dollar companies. Matt has been an Internet Marketer for over 14 years now and his techniques and strategies are widely used across the internet and he has taught many of the who's who of Internet Marketing. Many people say that Matt is a self-made millionaire. Matt says that is totally wrong. He says, he is a couple-made millionaire. "There is no way I could have gotten to the place I am today without my wife by my side." If you follow Matt on Twitter, Facebook and this blog you will realize that he is very devoted to his family.

Matt resides in Duluth, GA with his wife and three children (two girls and a boy). To find out more about Matt Bacak, go to

www.mattbacak.com

www.aboutmattbacak.com

Other titles by Matt Bacak

- **Marketing Sidekick**
- **Secrets of the Internet Millionaire Mind**
- **The Ultimate Lead Generation Plan**

If you would like to get your hands on the templates used inside this book, please go right now to
www.perfectcustomerbook.com/freetemplates

Made in the USA
Columbia, SC
22 October 2020